GORILLAS
Beasts of the Wild

Lucy Sackett Smith

PowerKiDS press™
New York

For Evan Power

Published in 2010 by The Rosen Publishing Group, Inc.
29 East 21st Street, New York, NY 10010

First Edition

Editor: Nicole Pristash
Book Design: Kate Laczynski
Photo Researcher: Jessica Gerweck

Photo Credits: Cover, p. 1 © www.istockphoto.com/Dave Barfield; pp. 5, 15 Michael Nichols/Getty Images; p. Andy Rouse/Getty Images; p. 9 © Markus Botzek/zefa/Corbis; pp. 10–11 Per-Anders Pettersson/Getty Image p. 13 © Yann Arthus-Bertrand/Corbis; p. 17 Frans Lanting/Corbis; p. 19 © Kevin Schafer/Corbis; p. 21 Jaso Edwards/Getty Images.

Library of Congress Cataloging-in-Publication Data

Smith, Lucy Sackett.
  Gorillas : beasts of the wild / Lucy Sackett Smith. — 1st ed.
    p. cm. — (Mighty mammals)
  Includes index.
  ISBN 978-1-4042-8104-2 (library binding) — ISBN 978-1-4358-3278-7 (pbk.) —
ISBN 978-1-4358-3279-4 (6-pack)
  1. Gorilla—Juvenile literature. I. Title.
  QL737.P96S583 2010
  599.884—dc22
                                                    2009000554

Manufactured in the United States of America

CONTENTS

Powerful Primates

Have you ever seen a gorilla in a movie or a TV show? Movies and shows often make these big **apes** seem like scary monsters that always want to fight. In truth, while gorillas are big and strong, they are generally peaceful.

Gorillas are Earth's biggest primates. Primates are a group of **mammals** that includes monkeys, lemurs, apes, and people. In fact, the gorilla is the animal that is most closely related to people. Gorillas are very smart animals. They use tools, they form close ties to other gorillas, and they have many ways of **communicating** with each other.

Gorillas are known for their strength. This gorilla is breaking tree branches so it can eat their soft insides.

Gorillas live in central Africa. **Scientists** break gorillas into two **species**. These species are the western gorilla and the eastern gorilla. Western gorillas make their homes in the thick, wet **rain forests** of central Africa. Some eastern gorillas live in rain forests, too. Other eastern gorillas live in the Virunga Mountains. These apes are found in thick, foggy mountain forests, called cloud forests.

Western gorillas have smaller ears and bigger brow, or forehead, **ridges** than their eastern relatives do. Western gorillas often have brownish gray coats, while eastern gorillas' coats are black. Gorillas from the Virunga Mountains generally have long hair.

These gorillas live in the Virunga Mountains where it is cool and wet. The gorillas' long, thick hair keeps them warm.

Giant Gorillas

Gorillas are large and powerful animals. Big male gorillas often weigh between 300 and 500 pounds (136–227 kg). Female gorillas are a bit smaller. They weigh between 150 and 200 pounds (68–91 kg).

When they walk, gorillas look hunched, or bent over. This is because a gorilla's arms are longer than its legs are. These apes sometimes stand up on two feet, as people do. However, gorillas most often walk on both their feet and their hands. Gorillas put their weight on their **knuckles** when they walk. Chimpanzees, gorillas' close relatives, also walk like this.

A gorilla walks on its hands by putting all of its weight on its knuckles as it moves.

MIGHTY FACTS

1. When they stand up, male gorillas are about 5.5 feet (2 m) tall. Females are generally about 5 feet (1.5 m) tall.

2. Though silverbacks will fight off other gorillas, they often avoid hitting their enemies. Silverbacks mostly try to scare enemies away by showing how big they are.

3. Gorillas have short, soft hair everywhere except on their faces and on the insides of their hands and feet.

4. You can tell any two gorillas apart by looking at their fingerprints. You can also use fingerprints to tell humans apart.

5. Gorillas can climb trees, but they spend most of their time on the ground. Young gorillas are found in trees more often than adults are.

6 Gorillas strengthen their ties with other gorillas by grooming, or cleaning, each other's coats.

7 Gorillas build a new nest each time they take a nap or settle down for a good night's sleep.

8 Gorillas can live as long as 35 years in the wild. In zoos, gorillas sometimes live into their 50s.

Smart Animals

Gorillas are very smart. Gorillas remember things well, and they are good at figuring out problems. Many scientists study gorillas because these apes are so closely related to people. Some people have studied gorillas in the wild. Scientists working in Africa have seen a gorilla use a stick to measure how deep the water was as the animal was walking through it.

Others scientists work with gorillas that are kept in zoos or labs. Scientists have taught more than 1,000 American **Sign Language** signs to a well-known gorilla, named Koko. Koko also understands several thousand words in English.

This man is studying gorillas in central Africa.
Gorillas are very smart, so there is a lot to learn from them.

Life in a Troop

Most wild gorillas are members of a troop, or group. Troops generally have between 2 and 30 gorillas. A troop's leader is an adult male, known as a silverback. Silverbacks get their name from the silverish gray hair on their backs. Troops also have younger males, called blackbacks. Several females and their babies are part of most troops, too.

Silverbacks decide where a troop will move and when it will stop for food. They guard the troop from other gorillas. If an unfriendly gorilla comes near, a silverback will stand up, scream, and beat its chest. Silverbacks also charge at enemies.

Here two large silverback gorillas (left) are shown leading their troop in a search for food in the Congo.

Gorillas Growing Up

Silverbacks control which male gorillas can **mate** with their troop's females. A silverback is often the father of all his troop's babies. Gorilla babies are born between eight and nine months after their mother and father mated. Newborn gorillas hang on tightly to their mothers and drink their milk. Young gorillas spend lots of time playing and learning new things.

When they reach about eight years old, female gorillas leave their troops to find a new troop. Young males also leave the troop in which they grew up. In time, these blackbacks become silverbacks and may lead troops of their own.

A baby gorilla learns to hang on to its mother's back when it is around four months old.

Hungry Apes

Each day, gorilla troops move around looking for food. Gorillas spend the morning moving from place to place and eating. In the afternoon, the adults often nap, while the children play. The apes eat again before settling down to sleep for the night.

Gorillas get a large amount of their food from plants. They like leaves, stems, fruits, and seeds. When hungry, these apes will even eat rotting wood! Gorillas also sometimes eat small animals, such as bugs. It takes a lot of food to feed a gorilla. Large male gorillas may eat as much as 40 pounds (18 kg) each day.

Gorillas have very strong mouths and teeth. This helps them chew through hard stems and leaves.

Bad News for Gorillas

Gorillas are so powerful that they have few **predators**. Leopards hunt gorillas from time to time but not very often. People are the biggest predator of gorillas. Some people hunt gorillas for their meat. Gorilla meat is known as bushmeat. Several African countries have made it against the law to kill gorillas. Sadly, hunters called poachers kill gorillas anyway.

For many years, gorillas were **protected** by the fact that the forests where they lived were hard to reach. However, people are now cutting down these forests. Gorillas are losing their homes, and it is now easier for poachers to find them.

If forests continue to be cut down, gorillas, like this one, will not have food to eat.

21

Protecting Gorillas

People have made so many problems for gorillas that these apes are in danger of dying out. However, people around the world are working to save these wonderful animals. People have set up gorilla reserves, which are places where land is set aside for gorillas to live in safety.

You can help gorillas by asking your mother or father and neighbors to buy certified wood. This is wood cut by companies that promise to follow laws protecting endangered animals, such as gorillas.

If we all work together, we can save the gorilla. The world is a more interesting place thanks to these smart and mighty apes!

GLOSSARY

apes (AYPS) Large animals that are relatives of people and monkeys.

communicating (kuh-MYOO-nih-kayt-ing) Sharing facts or feelings.

knuckles (NUH-kelz) The places where fingers bend.

mammals (MA-mulz) Warm-blooded animals that breathe air and feed milk to their young.

mate (MAYT) To come together to make babies.

predators (PREH-duh-terz) Animals that kill other animals for food.

protected (pruh-TEKT-ed) Kept safe.

rain forests (RAYN FOR-ests) Thick forests that get a large amount of rain during the year.

ridges (RIJ-ez) The long, narrow, upper parts of things.

scientists (SY-un-tists) People who study the world.

sign language (SYN LANG-gwij) A way of talking with hands that is used by people who cannot hear.

species (SPEE-sheez) One kind of living thing. All people are one species.

INDEX

WEB SITES

Due to the changing nature of Internet links, PowerKids Press has developed an online list of Web sites related to the subject of this book. This site is updated regularly. Please use this link to access the list: www.powerkidslinks.com/mamm/gorilla/